영어 리딩 학습의 핵심은 논픽션 독해력 향상에 있습니다.

학년이 올라갈수록 영어 시험 출제의 비중이 높아지는 논픽션. 우리는 논픽션 리딩을 통해 다양한 분야의 어휘와 지식을 습득하고 문제 해결 능력을 키울 수 있습니다. 또한 생활 속 실용문과 시험 상황의 복잡한 지문을 이해하고 분석하며, 나에게 필요한 정보를 추출하는 연습을 할 수 있습니다. 논픽션 독해력은 비판적 사고와 논리적 사고를 발전시키고, 영어로 표현된 아이디어를 깊이 있게 이해하고 효과적으로 소통하는 언어 능력을 갖출 수 있도록 도와줍니다.

미국교과서는 논픽션 리딩에 가장 적합한 학습 도구입니다.

미국교과서는 과학, 사회과학, 역사, 예술, 문학 등 다양한 주제의 폭넓은 지식과 이해를 제공하며, 사실을 그대로 받아들이는 능력뿐만 아니라 텍스트 너머의 맥락에 대한 비판적 사고와 분석 능력도 함께 배울 수 있도록 구성되어 있습니다. 미국 교과과정 주제의 리딩을 통해 학생들은 현실적인 주제를 탐구하고, 아카데믹한 어휘를 학습하면서 논리적 탐구의 방법을 함께 배울 수 있습니다. 미국교과서는 논픽션 독해력 향상을 위한 최고의 텍스트입니다.

탁월한 논픽션 독해력을 원한다면
미국교과서 READING 시리즈

① 미국교과서의 핵심 주제들을 엄선하여 담은 지문을 읽으며 **독해력**이 향상되고 **배경지식**이 쌓입니다.

② 가지고 있는 지식과 새로운 정보를 연결해 내 것으로 만드는 **통합사고력**을 기를 수 있습니다.

③ 꼼꼼히 읽고 완전히 소화할 수 있도록 하는 수준별 독해 훈련으로 **문제 해결력**이 향상됩니다.

④ 기초 문장 독해에서 추론까지, 학습자의 **수준별로 선택하여 학습**할 수 있도록 난이도를 설계하였습니다.

⑤ 스스로 계획하고 점검하며 실력을 쌓아가는 **자기주도력**이 형성됩니다.

Author Contents Tree

Contents Tree has published various English learning textbooks and teacher's guides. It also provides an English Reading Specialist Training Course for English teachers. At the same time, Contents Tree runs an English Reading Library named Reader's Mate.

미국교과서 **READING LEVEL 1 ❸**
American Textbook Reading *Second Edition*

Second Published on August 14, 2023
Second Printed on August 30, 2023

First Published on July 18, 2016

Written by Contents Tree
Editorial Manager Namhui Kim, Seulgi Han
Development Editor Mina Park
Proofreading Ryan P. Lagace, Benjamin Schultz
Design Kichun Jang, Hyeonsook Lee
Typesetting Yeon Design
Illustrations Eunhyung Ryu, Heeju Joe
Recording Studio YR Media
Photo Credit Photos.com, Shutterstcok.com

Published and distributed by Gilbutschool

56, Worldcup-ro 10-gil, Mapo-gu, Seoul, Korea, 121-842
Tel 02-332-0931
Fax 02-322-0586
Homepage www.gilbutschool.co.kr
Publisher Jongwon Lee

ISBN   979-11-6406-540-0 (64740)
         979-11-6406-535-6 (set)
(Gilbutschool code : 30538)

미국교과서 리딩

READING

LEVEL 1 ③

길벗스쿨

★ 이 책의 특징 ★

LEVEL 1 논픽션 리딩 준비

리딩의 기초가 되는 언어 실력을 키울 수 있는 학습 요소를 중점적으로 익힙니다.

영어 학습의 기초 능력을 다지는 시기로서 지문에 등장할 어휘를 미리 숙지하고 패턴 문형을 반복적으로 눈과 귀로 익혀, 리딩을 수월히 소화할 수 있도록 구성하였습니다.

미국 프리스쿨 과정의 일상 주제와 기초 논픽션 주제 어휘를 학습합니다.

● 권별 주제 구성

1권	2권	3권
1. Body Parts	13. Rain	25. Tree
2. My Brother	14. Spring	26. Housework
3. Family	15. Things in Pairs	27. Riding a Bike
4. My School	16. Animal Homes	28. Spider
5. Animals	17. Community	29. Hobbies
6. Seasons	18. My Room	30. Winter
7. Things in the Sky	19. Bad Dream	31. Vegetables
8. Shapes	20. Colors	32. Sea
9. Clothes	21. Food	33. My Town
10. Monsters	22. Transportation	34. School Tools
11. Jobs	23. Friends	35. Farm Animals
12. Museum	24. Sense of Touch	36. Five Senses

필수 패턴 문형이 반복되는 지문을 읽으며 문장 구조에 익숙해집니다.

글의 주제와 가벼운 의미 파악 수준의 기초 독해 연습으로 리딩의 기본기를 만듭니다.

	Study Check		Day			Study Check		Day
Unit 1	Get Ready	☐	/		**Unit 7**	Get Ready	☐	/
	Now You Read	☐	/			Now You Read	☐	/
	Check Up	☐	/			Check Up	☐	/
	Workbook	☐	/			Workbook	☐	/
Unit 2	Get Ready	☐	/		**Unit 8**	Get Ready	☐	/
	Now You Read	☐	/			Now You Read	☐	/
	Check Up	☐	/			Check Up	☐	/
	Workbook	☐	/			Workbook	☐	/
Unit 3	Get Ready	☐	/		**Unit 9**	Get Ready	☐	/
	Now You Read	☐	/			Now You Read	☐	/
	Check Up	☐	/			Check Up	☐	/
	Workbook	☐	/			Workbook	☐	/
Unit 4	Get Ready	☐	/		**Unit 10**	Get Ready	☐	/
	Now You Read	☐	/			Now You Read	☐	/
	Check Up	☐	/			Check Up	☐	/
	Workbook	☐	/			Workbook	☐	/
Unit 5	Get Ready	☐	/		**Unit 11**	Get Ready	☐	/
	Now You Read	☐	/			Now You Read	☐	/
	Check Up	☐	/			Check Up	☐	/
	Workbook	☐	/			Workbook	☐	/
Unit 6	Get Ready	☐	/		**Unit 12**	Get Ready	☐	/
	Now You Read	☐	/			Now You Read	☐	/
	Check Up	☐	/			Check Up	☐	/
	Workbook	☐	/			Workbook	☐	/

Get Ready

기초 단어와 핵심 패턴 문형을 익히며 글의 소재를 알아보고,
문장 구조에 익숙해집니다.

QR코드를 스캔하여 정확한 발음 확인하기

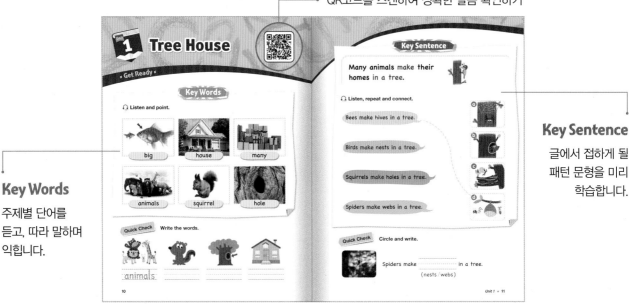

Key Words

주제별 단어를
듣고, 따라 말하며
익힙니다.

Key Sentence

글에서 접하게 될
패턴 문형을 미리
학습합니다.

Now You Read

일상생활, 학교생활 주제의 글을 읽으며 기초 독해력을 쌓고,
어휘와 문장에 익숙해집니다.

Reading Passage

그림을 통해 내용을
먼저 예측해 본 후,
음원을 듣고, 따라
읽으며 세부 내용을
파악합니다.

Pop Quiz

그림, 사진 관련
퀴즈를 풀며 글의
내용을 다시 한 번
떠올려 봅니다.

Check Up

다양한 유형의 문제를 풀며 읽은 내용을 확인하고,
단어와 문장을 점검합니다.

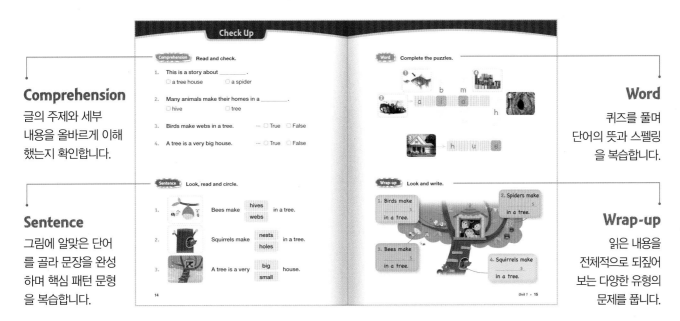

Comprehension
글의 주제와 세부
내용을 올바르게 이해
했는지 확인합니다.

Sentence
그림에 알맞은 단어
를 골라 문장을 완성
하며 핵심 패턴 문형
을 복습합니다.

Word
퀴즈를 풀며
단어의 뜻과 스펠링
을 복습합니다.

Wrap-up
읽은 내용을
전체적으로 되짚어
보는 다양한 유형의
문제를 풉니다.

Workbook

단어와 패턴 문형을
복습합니다.

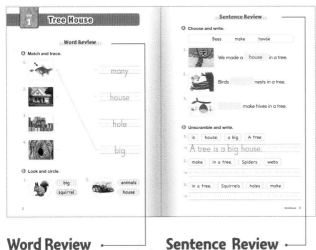

Word Review
단어의 의미를 확인하고
쓰면서 복습합니다.

Sentence Review
문장 완성하기, 순서 배열하기
활동으로 패턴 문형과 어순을
복습합니다.

무료 온라인 학습 자료

길벗스쿨 e클래스
(eclass.gilbut.co.kr)에
접속하시면 〈미국교과서
READING〉 시리즈에 대한
상세 정보 및 부가 학습 자료를
무료로 이용하실 수 있습니다.

1. 음원 스트리밍 및 MP3 파일
2. 추가 학습용 워크시트 5종
   단어 카드, 단어 테스트, 문장 따라 쓰기,
   리딩 지문 테스트, 문장 테스트
3. 복습용 온라인 퀴즈

★ 목차 ★

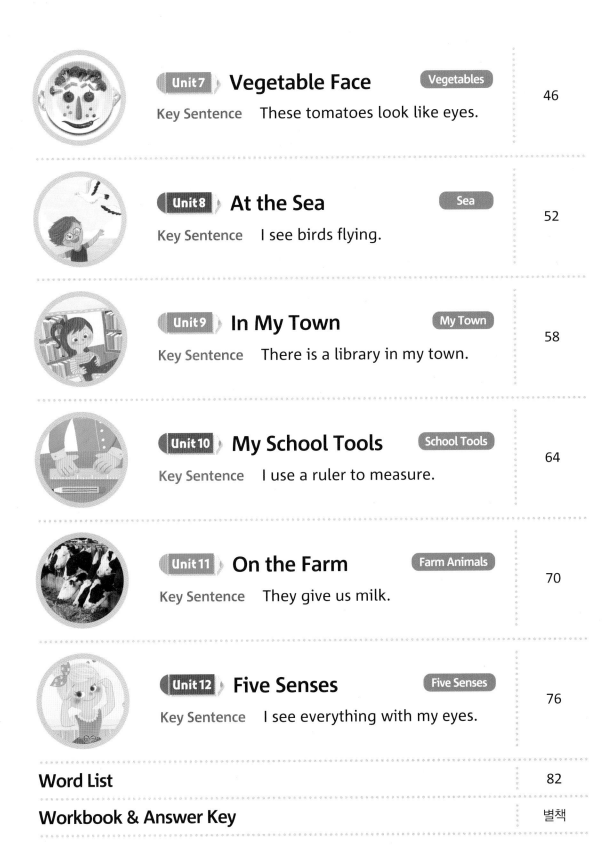

Tree House

▪ Get Ready ▪

Key Words

🎧 **Listen and point.**

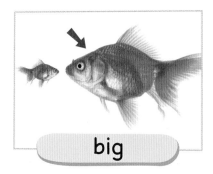

big

house

many

animals

squirrel

hole

Quick Check **Write the words.**

animals

Key Sentence

Many animals make their homes in a tree.

🎧 **Listen, repeat and connect.**

Bees **make** hives **in a tree.**

Birds **make** nests **in a tree.**

Squirrels **make** holes **in a tree.**

Spiders **make** webs **in a tree.**

Quick Check   **Circle and write.**

Spiders make ⎯⎯⎯⎯⎯⎯⎯⎯⎯ in a tree.

(nests / webs)

Tree House

A tree is a big house.

Many animals **make** their homes **in a tree**.

Bees **make** hives **in a tree**.

Birds **make** nests **in a tree**.

Squirrels **make** holes **in a tree**.

Spiders **make** webs **in a tree**.

Look, we **made** a house **in a tree**, too.

A tree is a very big house.

Check Up

 **Read and check.**

1. This is a story about _____ .

   ☐ a tree house   ☐ a spider

2. Many animals make their homes in a _____ .

   ☐ hive   ☐ tree

3. Birds make webs in a tree.   ··· ☐ True   ☐ False

4. A tree is a very big house.   ··· ☐ True   ☐ False

 **Look, read and circle.**

1.    Bees make   hives / webs   in a tree.

2.    Squirrels make   nests / holes   in a tree.

3.    A tree is a very   big / small   house.

Complete the puzzles.

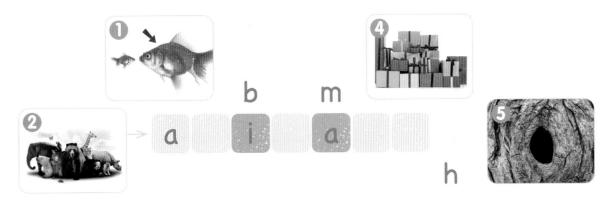

Wrap-up   Look and write.

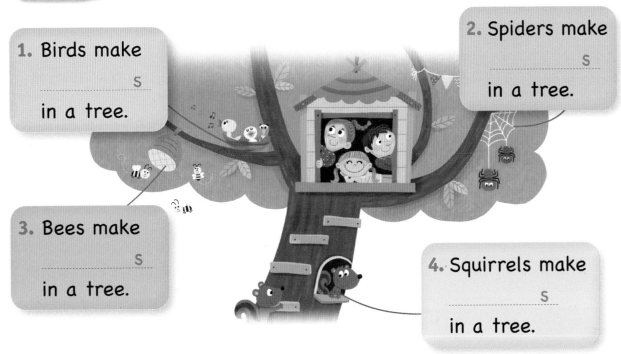

1. Birds make
_____ s
in a tree.

2. Spiders make
_____ s
in a tree.

3. Bees make
_____ s
in a tree.

4. Squirrels make
_____ s
in a tree.

Get Ready

Key Words

🎧 Listen and point.

clean

bedroom

bathroom

mirror

kitchen

living room

Quick Check Write the words.

_____

_____

_____

_____

Mom cleans **the bedroom.**

🎧 **Listen, repeat and connect.**

Dad cleans the bathroom.

He cleans the floor.

She cleans the living room.

I clean the kitchen.

Quick Check **Circle and write.**

Dad cleans the _____ .

(bedroom / bathroom)

Cleaning Day 🎧

It is Sunday morning.

We are busy today.

Mom cleans the bedroom.

She makes the bed.

Dad cleans the bathroom.

He wipes the mirror.

We help Mom and Dad.

I clean the kitchen.

I do the dishes.

Jack cleans the living room.

He mops the floor.

Now, our house is clean!

Pop Quiz

What animal lives in this house?

 **Read and check.**

1. This is a story about _____ .

   ☐ cleaning   ☐ moving

2. We are _____ today.

   ☐ happy   ☐ busy

3. Dad cleans the bathroom.   ⋯ ☐ True   ☐ False

4. Mom does the dishes.   ⋯ ☐ True   ☐ False

 **Look, read and circle.**

1.    I clean the   kitchen   .
                                         bedroom

2.    Jack cleans the   mirror   .
                                            living room

3.    Now, our house is   clean   !
                                              messy

Find and circle.

bathroom

mirror

b	a	t	h	r	o	o	m
c	d	e	m	n	b	o	i
v	c	l	e	a	n	s	r
b	g	d	r	o	a	m	r
p	t	o	u	y	i	m	o
k	i	t	c	h	e	n	r

clean

kitchen

Wrap-up **Write and match.**

1.  Dad cleans the _____ .

2. Mom cleans the _____ .

3. I clean the _____ .

4. Jack cleans the _____ .

ⓐ She makes the bed.

ⓑ He wipes the mirror.

ⓒ He mops the floor.

ⓓ I do the dishes.

Unit 3 Safe Riding

Key Words

🎧 **Listen and point.**

ride

bike

safety

helmet

knee pads

lights

Quick Check   Write the words.

_____

_____

_____

_____

Put on your helmet.

🎧 **Listen, repeat and connect.**

Put on your knee pads.

Stop at a red light.

Cross at a green light.

Follow the traffic lights.

Quick Check   Circle and write.

Put on your _____ .

(helmet / knee pads)

Safe Riding

Let's ride our bikes today.

Don't forget the safety rules.

Put on your helmet.

It protects your head.

Put on your knee pads.

They protect your knees.

24

Follow the traffic lights.

They keep you safe.

Stop at a red light.

Cross at a green light.

Pop Quiz

How many cars are on the road?

Oh, Dad!
Watch out!

 **Comprehension** **Read and check.**

1. This is a story about _____.

   ☐ safe riding ☐ safe swimming

2. Don't forget the safety _____.

   ☐ nest ☐ rules

3. The helmet protects your head. ··· ☐ True ☐ False

4. The knee pads protect your hands. ··· ☐ True ☐ False

 **Sentence** **Look, read and circle.**

1. Let's ride our | bikes / sleds | today.

2. Put on your | knee pads / helmet |.

3. Stop at a | red / green | light.

Word Complete the puzzles.

① k e p d s

② l g t s

③ h ... r ... e ... m

④

⑤ b e

Wrap-up Match and write.

1. They keep you safe.

2. It protects your head.

3. They protect your knees.

a

b

c .... traffic

Is a Spider an Insect?

▪ Get Ready ▪

Key Words

🎧 **Listen and point.**

insects

three

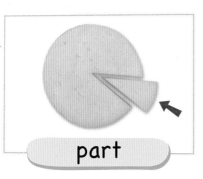

part

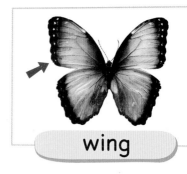

wing

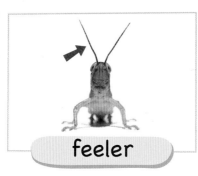

feeler

think

Quick Check   **Write the words.**

_____   _____   _____   _____

A spider has **two body parts.**

🎧 **Listen, repeat and connect.**

An insect has six legs.

An insect has wings.

An insect has three body parts.

A spider has eight legs.

Quick Check   Circle and write.

An insect has _____ .

(wings / knees)

Is a Spider an Insect?

An insect has three body parts.

A spider has two body parts.

An insect has wings.

A spider has no wings.

An **insect has** six legs.

A **spider has** eight legs.

An **insect has** feelers.

A **spider has** no feelers.

Do you think a spider is an insect?

Pop Quiz

What animal is on the web?

Comprehension Read and check.

1. This is a story about _____ .

   ☐ a spider   ☐ a butterfly

2. A spider has _____ body parts.

   ☐ two   ☐ three

3. An insect has three body parts.   ⋯ ☐ True   ☐ False

4. A spider is an insect.   ⋯ ☐ True   ☐ False

Sentence Look, read and circle.

1.  An insect has wings / hands .

2.  A spider has eight feelers / legs .

3.  Do you think / make a spider is an insect?

Find and circle.

insects

feeler

t	a	m	f	f	e	b	c
h	j	p	e	e	x	z	w
i	n	s	e	c	t	s	a
n	t	q	l	l	x	d	b
k	g	q	e	e	e	g	c
o	p	a	r	t	c	i	m

think

part

Wrap-up **Look and match.**

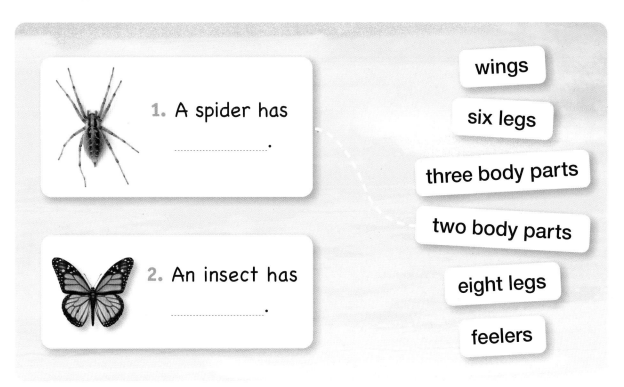

1. A spider has _____.

2. An insect has _____.

wings

six legs

three body parts

two body parts

eight legs

feelers

Key Words

🎧 **Listen and point.**

hobby

cook

story

picture

collect

key

Quick Check   Write the words.

_____ _____ _____ _____

Key Sentence

He likes to **cook eggs**.

🎧 **Listen, repeat and connect.**

She likes to write stories.

He likes to draw pictures.

He likes to read books.

I like to collect key rings.

Quick Check Circle and write.

She likes to write _____ .

(pictures / stories)

Different Hobbies

Everyone has hobbies.

They bring us joy.

Jimmy enjoys cooking.

He likes to cook eggs.

Anna enjoys writing.

She likes to write stories.

David enjoys drawing.

He likes to draw pictures.

I enjoy collecting.

I like to collect key rings.

We have different hobbies.

What are your hobbies?

 **Read and check.**

1. This is a story about _____ .

   ☐ hobbies   ☐ pictures

2. Hobbies bring us _____ .

   ☐ safety   ☐ joy

3. Jimmy enjoys writing.   ⋯ ☐ True   ☐ False

4. We have different hobbies.   ⋯ ☐ True   ☐ False

 **Look, read and circle.**

1. Anna likes to write   stories

   key rings .

2. David enjoys   cooking

   drawing .

3. I like to   collect   key rings.

   cook

Complete the puzzle.

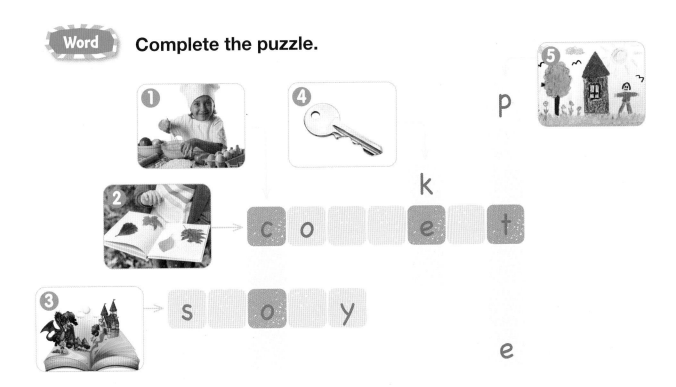

Wrap-up **Look and write.**

1. Jimmy likes to _____ eggs.

2. David likes to _____ pictures.

3. I like to _____ key rings.

4. Anna likes to _____ stories.

Key Words

🎧 **Listen and point.**

sled

snowman

listen

long

scary

give

Quick Check   Write the words.

Winter is for riding.

🎧 **Listen, repeat and connect.**

Winter is for building.

Winter is for listening.

Winter is for giving.

Winter is for skating.

Quick Check   Circle and write.

Winter is for _____ .

(listening / building)

Winter Fun

Winter is for riding.

We sled down the hill.

We sled all day long.

Winter is for building.

We have lots of snow.

We build a snowman.

Winter is for listening.

The nights are long.

We listen to scary stories.

Winter is for giving.

Christmas is in winter.

We give gifts to friends.

Winter is so much fun!

Pop Quiz

What is the snowman wearing?

Comprehension Read and check.

1. This is a story about _____ .
   ☐ snow   ☐ winter

2. We _____ all day long.
   ☐ sled   ☐ sleep

3. Winter is for building.   ··· ☐ True   ☐ False

4. The nights are short in winter.   ··· ☐ True   ☐ False

Sentence Look, read and circle.

1.  Winter is for | listening |
                                        | singing | .

2.  We build a | snowman |
                                    | house | .

3.  Winter is for | giving |
                                        | riding | .

Find and circle.

give

sled

s	b	a	d	a	m	l	e
c	o	e	e	w	f	e	v
a	r	t	s	c	a	t	s
r	g	i	v	e	p	a	f
y	o	r	w	s	l	e	d
s	n	o	w	m	a	n	s

scary

snowman

Wrap-up **Look and write.**

1. We build a _____ .

2. We listen to _____ stories.

3. We _____ all day long.

Winter is so much fun!

4. We _____ gifts to friends.

Unit 7 Vegetable Face

vegetables

broccoli

hair

carrot

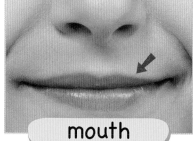
mouth

health

Get Ready

Key Words

🎧 **Listen and point.**

Quick Check Write the words.

_____
- - - - - - - - - -
_____

_____
- - - - - - - - - -
_____

_____
- - - - - - - - - -
_____

_____
- - - - - - - - - -
_____

These tomatoes look like eyes.

🎧 **Listen, repeat and connect.**

a

These broccoli **look like** hair.

b

This corn **looks like** teeth.

c

This pepper **looks like** a mouth.

d

This carrot **looks like** a nose.

Quick Check **Circle and write.**

This carrot looks like a _____ .

(nose / mouth)

Vegetable Face 🎧

Do you like vegetables?

You don't like vegetables?

No.

Vegetables are good
for your health.
And they look funny!

48

Look! Here is my artwork!

These tomatoes **look like** eyes.

These broccoli **look like** hair.

This carrot **looks like** a nose.

This pepper **looks like** a mouth.

I like vegetables so much!

 **Read and check.**

1. This is a story about _____.

   ☐ vegetables   ☐ faces

2. Vegetables are good for your _____.

   ☐ house   ☐ health

3. These tomatoes look like a nose.   ··· ☐ True   ☐ False

4. This pepper looks like a mouth.   ··· ☐ True   ☐ False

 **Look, read and circle.**

1. This carrot looks like a   nose / mouth .

2. These broccoli look like   eyes / hair .

3. Vegetables look   scary / funny !

Complete the puzzle.

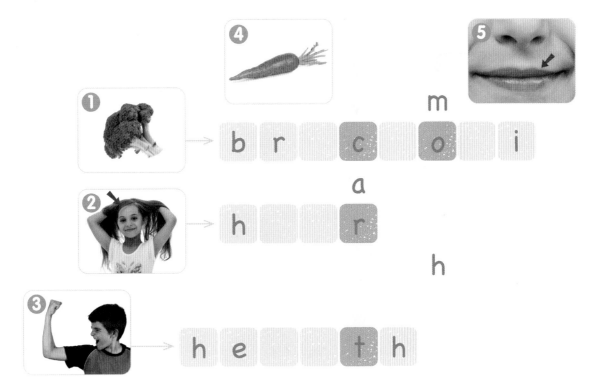

④

⑤

①

②

③

| b | r | | c | | o | | i |

m

| h | | | r |

a

| h | e | | | t | h |

h

   **Look and write.**

1. These _____ look like hair.

2. These _____ look like eyes.

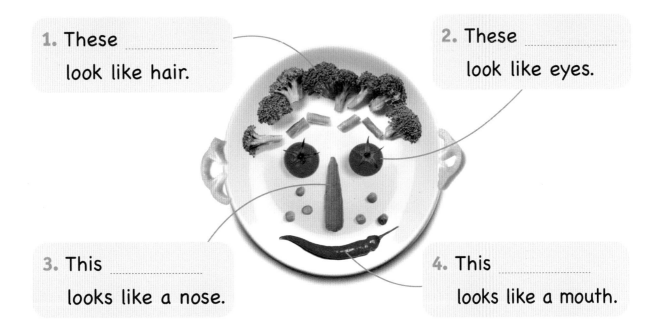

3. This _____ looks like a nose.

4. This _____ looks like a mouth.

Unit 8 At the Sea

Key Words

🎧 **Listen and point.**

sea

turtle

crawl

sand

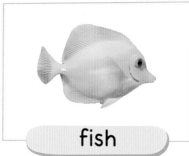
fish

crab

Quick Check   Write the words.

_____   _____   _____   _____

Key Sentence

I see **birds fly**ing.

🎧 **Listen, repeat and connect.**

I see turtles crawling.

a

I see fish swimming.

b

I see crabs walking sideways.

c

I see clouds moving.

d

Quick Check   **Circle and write.**

I see turtles _____ .

(swimming / crawling)

At the Sea 🎧

I see many things at the sea.

I do many things at the sea.

I see birds fly**ing**.

I fly in the air, too.

I see turtles crawl**ing**.

I crawl in the sand, too.

I see fish swimm**ing**.

I swim in the water, too.

Pop Quiz

How many seashells can you see?

I see crabs walk**ing** sideways.

I walk sideways, too.

Ouch!

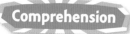 **Comprehension**   **Read and check.**

1. This is a story about many things at the _____ .

   ☐ hill   ☐ sea

2. I see birds _____ .

   ☐ flying   ☐ running

3. I do many things at the sea.   ··· ☐ True ☐ False

4. I fly in the water, too.   ··· ☐ True ☐ False

Sentence   **Look, read and circle.**

1.    I see fish

        crawling

        swimming   .

2.    I crawl in the

        sand

        air   , too.

3.    I see

        crabs

        birds   walking sideways.

Word Find and circle.

crawl

sand

g	i	w	d	c	r	a	b
t	j	s	d	r	x	c	n
h	d	c	s	a	n	d	q
s	a	n	o	w	d	p	o
e	w	f	a	l	x	v	a
a	i	o	w	s	x	c	n

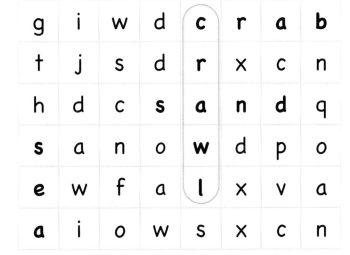

sea

crab

Wrap-up Match and write.

1.

2.

3.

4.

a. I see crabs _____ sideways.

b. I see birds _____ .

c. I see turtles _____ .

d. I see fish _____ .

In My Town

Get Ready

Key Words

🎧 **Listen and point.**

library

town

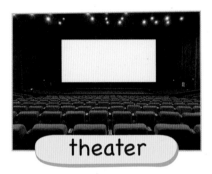
theater

watch

park

pool

Quick Check   Write the words.

_____   _____   _____   _____

Key Sentence

There is **a library** in my town.

🎧 **Listen, repeat and connect.**

There is a theater **in my town.**

There is a park in my town.

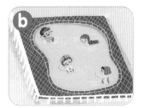

There is a swimming pool in my town.

There is a museum **in my town.**

Quick Check Circle and write.

There is a _____ in my town.

(library / theater)

In My Town 🎧

There is a library **in my town**.

I read books in the library.

There is a theater **in my town**.

I watch movies in the theater.

60

There is a park **in my town**.

I ride my bike in the park.

Pop Quiz

How many kids are swimming in the pool?

There is a swimming pool **in my town**.

I swim in the pool every day.

What places are there in your town?

 **Read and check.**

1. This is a story about _____.
   ☐ my house ☐ my town

2. I read books in the _____.
   ☐ library ☐ swimming pool

3. There is a park in my town. ··· ☐ True ☐ False

4. I swim in the theater. ··· ☐ True ☐ False

 **Look, read and circle.**

1.  There is a
   park
   library
   in my town.

2.  There is a
   swimming pool
   theater
   in my town.

3.  I ride my
   bike
   bus
   in the park.

Complete the puzzles.

t [ ] w [ ]

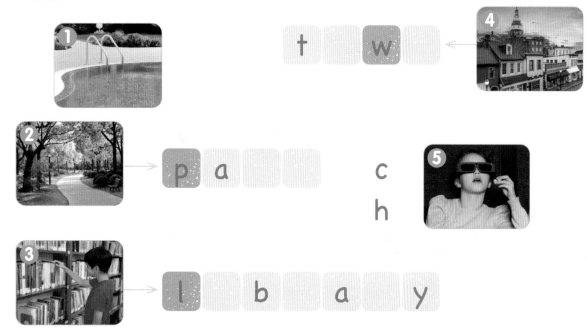

p a [ ] [ ]   c
                h

l [ ] b [ ] a [ ] y

Wrap-up   **Match and write.**

1. I watch movies in the _____.

2. I swim in the _____.

3. I read books in the _____.

4. I ride my bike in the _____.

Unit 10 My School Tools

Key Words

🎧 **Listen and point.**

tools

ruler

crayons

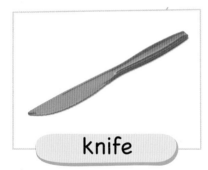
knife

fork

cup

Quick Check **Write the words.**

_____ _____ _____ _____

Key Sentence

I use a ruler to measure.

🎧 **Listen, repeat and connect.**

I use a pencil **to** write.

I use crayons **to** color.

I use a knife **to** cut.

I use a cup **to** drink.

Quick Check Circle and write.

I use a _____ to measure.

(knife / ruler)

Unit 10 ▪ 65

My School Tools 🎧

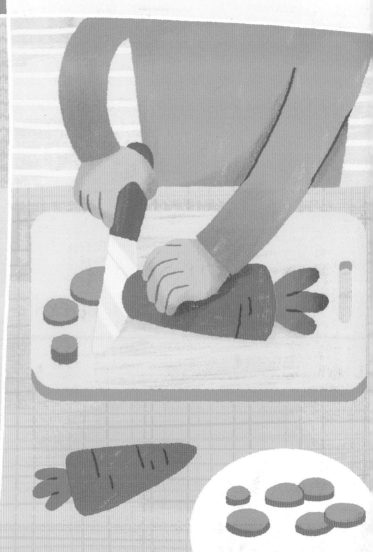

I use tools at school every day.

In math class, **I use** a ruler **to** measure.

In writing class, **I use** a pencil **to** write.

In art class, **I use** crayons **to** color.

In cooking class, **I use** a knife **to** cut.

At lunch time, I use many tools, too.

I use a fork **to** eat.

I use a cup **to** drink.

 **Comprehension**   Read and check.

1. This is a story about _____ .

   ☐ school tools   ☐ classes

2. I use tools at _____ every day.

   ☐ the park   ☐ school

3. I use a ruler to measure.   ⋯ ☐ True   ☐ False

4. I use crayons to cut.   ⋯ ☐ True   ☐ False

Sentence   Look, read and circle.

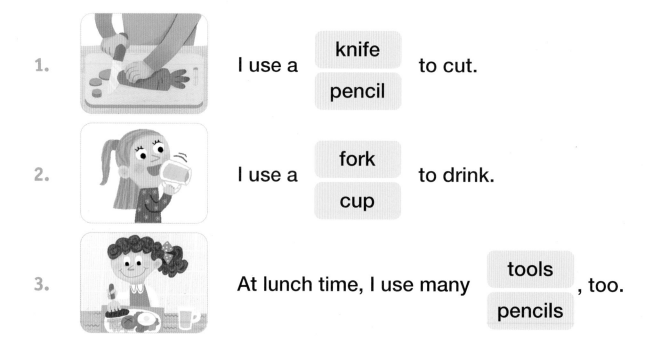

1. I use a   knife / pencil   to cut.

2. I use a   fork / cup   to drink.

3. At lunch time, I use many   tools / pencils , too.

crayons

knife

k	n	i	f	e	c	p	t
z	x	n	b	f	h	p	o
x	a	p	c	x	p	c	o
p	a	b	u	l	t	r	l
x	t	v	p	v	b	y	s
c	r	a	y	o	n	s	n

tools

cup

Wrap-up   **Write and match.**

1.    I use _____

2. I use a _____

3. I use a _____

4. I use a _____

ⓐ to eat.

ⓑ to drink.

ⓒ to color.

ⓓ to write.

On the Farm

Key Words

🎧 **Listen and point.**

raise

cheese

duck

feather

sheep

wool

Quick Check   Write the words.

_____

_____

_____

_____

Key Sentence

They give us milk.

🎧 **Listen, repeat and connect.**

They give us cheese.

They give us fresh eggs.

They give us nice feathers.

They give us cozy wool.

Quick Check   Circle and write.

They give us fresh _____ .

(eggs / cheese)

On the Farm 🎧

We are a farm family.

We raise many animals on the farm.

My father raises cows.

They give us

milk and cheese.

My mother raises hens.
They give us fresh eggs.

Pop Quiz

How many eggs can you see?

My aunt raises sheep.
They give us cozy wool.

And I raise ducks.
They give us nice feathers.

We live on a farm with many animals.

Comprehension **Read and check.**

1. This is a story about _____ .

    ☐ food   ☐ a farm

2. We _____ many animals on the farm.

    ☐ raise   ☐ give

3. My father raises cows.   ⋯ ☐ True   ☐ False

4. We live in the city.   ⋯ ☐ True   ☐ False

Sentence **Look, read and circle.**

1.  Ducks give us nice milk / feathers .

2.  My aunt raises sheep / hens .

3.  Cows give us wool / cheese .

Word Complete the puzzles.

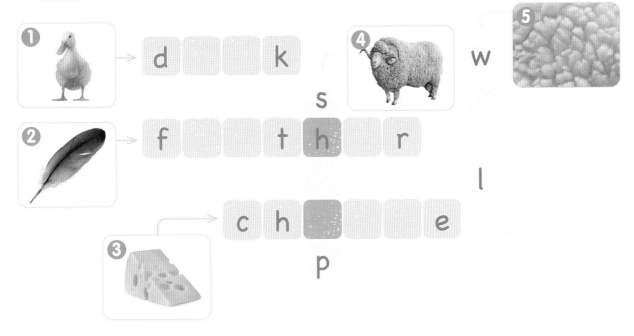

① d ☐ ☐ k

② f ☐ ☐ ☐ t **h** ☐ r

s

④ w

⑤

③ c h ☐ ☐ ☐ e

p

l

Wrap-up Match and write.

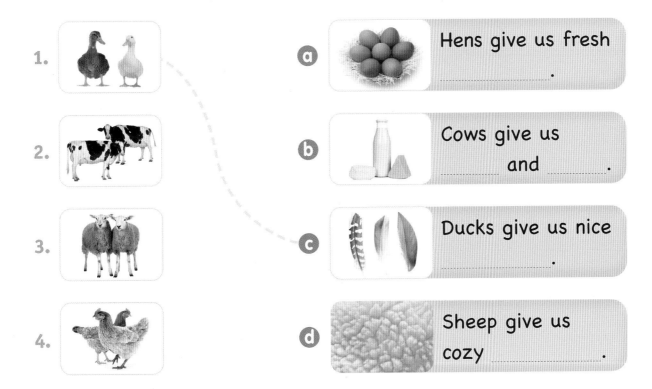

1.

2.

3.

4.

ⓐ Hens give us fresh
_____.

ⓑ Cows give us
_____ and _____.

ⓒ Ducks give us nice
_____.

ⓓ Sheep give us
cozy _____.

Five Senses

Key Words

🎧 Listen and point.

hear

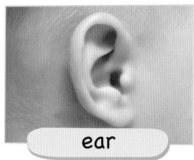

ear

smell

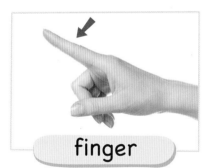

finger

taste

sweet

Quick Check   Write the words.

_____

_____

I see everything with my eyes.

🎧 **Listen, repeat and connect.**

I **hear** everything **with** my ears.

I **smell** everything **with** my nose.

I **touch** everything **with** my fingers.

I **taste** everything **with** my tongue.

Quick Check   Circle and write.

I _____ everything with my tongue.

(taste / hear)

Five Senses

I see everything **with** my eyes.

I see my grandma smiling.

I hear everything **with** my ears.

I hear my brother laughing.

I smell everything **with** my nose.

I smell my mom baking bread.

I touch everything **with** my fingers.

I touch my dad's beard.

I taste everything **with** my tongue.

I taste my mom's sweet cake.

Pop Quiz

What fruit is there on the cake?

 **Comprehension**　**Read and check.**

1.　This is a story about five _____ .

　　☐ senses　　　　　☐ fingers

2.　I see everything with my _____ .

　　☐ ears　　　　　　☐ eyes

3.　I hear my brother laughing.　　⋯ ☐ True　☐ False

4.　I smell everything with my eyes.　⋯ ☐ True　☐ False

 **Sentence**　**Look, read and circle.**

1.　I taste everything with my 　nose / tongue 　.

2.　 I touch everything with my 　fingers / ears 　.

3.　I 　see / smell 　my mom baking bread.

Word Find and circle.

sweet

smell

s	w	e	e	t	s	o	x
e	b	s	d	e	m	n	g
b	f	i	n	g	e	r	c
x	e	b	c	d	l	w	e
p	d	e	d	n	l	w	a
h	a	s	t	a	w	d	r

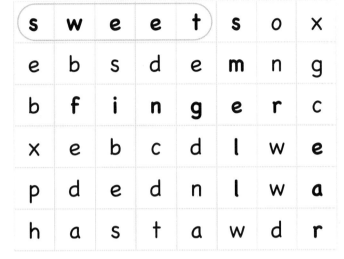

finger

ear

Wrap-up Look and write.

1. I _____ everything with my fingers.

2. I _____ everything with my eyes.

3. I _____ everything with my ears.

4. I _____ everything with my nose.

5. I _____ everything with my tongue.

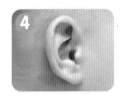

WORD LIST

- [ ] animal   동물
- [ ] bee   벌
- [ ] big   큰
- [ ] bird   새
- [ ] hive   벌집
- [ ] hole   구멍
- [ ] house   집
- [ ] make   만들다
- [ ] many   많은
- [ ] nest   (새의) 둥지
- [ ] spider   거미
- [ ] squirrel   다람쥐
- [ ] tree   나무
- [ ] web   거미줄

- [ ] bathroom   욕실, 화장실
- [ ] bedroom   침실
- [ ] busy   바쁜
- [ ] clean   청소하다; 깨끗한
- [ ] dish   접시
- [ ] do the dishes   설거지하다
- [ ] floor   바닥
- [ ] help   돕다
- [ ] kitchen   부엌
- [ ] living room   거실
- [ ] make the bed   침대를 정리하다
- [ ] mirror   거울
- [ ] mop   대걸레로 닦다
- [ ] morning   아침
- [ ] Sunday   일요일
- [ ] today   오늘
- [ ] wipe   닦다

- [ ] bike   자전거
- [ ] cross   건너다
- [ ] follow   (지시 등을) 따르다
- [ ] forget   잊다, 잊어버리다
- [ ] helmet   헬멧
- [ ] keep   유지하다
- [ ] knee pads   무릎 보호대
- [ ] light   신호등, 불빛
- [ ] protect   보호하다
- [ ] put on   ~을 입다, 착용하다
- [ ] ride   (자전거 등을) 타다

☐ rule	규칙
☐ safe	안전한
☐ safety	안전
☐ stop	멈추다, 그만하다
☐ traffic lights	신호등
☐ watch out	조심하다

· Unit 4 ·
Is a Spider an Insect?

☐ feeler	더듬이
☐ insect	곤충
☐ leg	다리
☐ part	부분
☐ think	생각하다
☐ three	3, 셋
☐ wing	날개

· Unit 5 ·
Different Hobbies

☐ bring	가져다주다
☐ collect	모으다
☐ cook	요리하다; 요리사
☐ different	다른, 여러 가지의
☐ draw	그리다
☐ enjoy	즐기다
☐ hobby	취미

☐ joy	기쁨, 즐거움
☐ key	열쇠
☐ key ring	열쇠고리
☐ picture	그림, 사진
☐ read	읽다
☐ story	이야기
☐ write	쓰다

· Unit 6 ·
Winter Fun

☐ all day long	하루 종일
☐ build	만들다, 짓다
☐ fun	재미; 재미있는
☐ gift	선물
☐ give	주다
☐ hill	언덕
☐ listen	듣다
☐ long	긴
☐ night	밤
☐ scary	무서운
☐ skate	스케이트를 타다
☐ sled	썰매; 썰매를 타다
☐ snow	눈; 눈이 오다
☐ snowman	눈사람
☐ winter	겨울

· Unit 7 ·
Vegetable Face

☐ broccoli	브로콜리
☐ carrot	당근
☐ corn	옥수수
☐ eye	눈
☐ face	얼굴
☐ funny	재미있는
☐ hair	머리카락
☐ health	건강
☐ look like	～처럼 보이다
☐ mouth	입
☐ nose	코
☐ pepper	고추
☐ teeth	이, 치아 (tooth의 복수형)
☐ tomato	토마토
☐ vegetable	채소

· Unit 8 ·
At the Sea

☐ crab	게
☐ crawl	기어가다
☐ fish	물고기
☐ sand	모래
☐ sea	바다

☐ sideways	옆으로	☐ drink	마시다; 음료	☐ sheep	양
☐ swim	수영하다	☐ fork	포크	☐ uncle	삼촌, 고모부, 이모부
☐ turtle	거북이	☐ knife	칼	☐ wool	양털
☐ walk	걷다	☐ lunch	점심 식사		

☐ drink	마시다; 음료
☐ fork	포크
☐ knife	칼
☐ lunch	점심 식사
☐ math	수학
☐ measure	측정하다, 재다
☐ pencil	연필
☐ ruler	자
☐ school	학교
☐ tool	도구
☐ use	사용하다

· Unit 9 ·
In My Town

☐ library	도서관
☐ movie	영화
☐ museum	박물관
☐ park	공원
☐ place	장소
☐ pool	수영장
☐ swimming pool	수영장
☐ theater	극장
☐ town	동네, 마을
☐ watch	보다

· Unit 10 ·
My School Tools

☐ art	미술
☐ class	수업
☐ color	색칠하다; 색깔
☐ crayon	크레용
☐ cup	컵
☐ cut	자르다

· Unit 11 ·
On the Farm

☐ aunt	이모, 고모, 숙모
☐ cheese	치즈
☐ cozy	포근한
☐ duck	오리
☐ egg	달걀
☐ farm	농장
☐ feather	깃털
☐ fresh	신선한
☐ hen	암탉
☐ live	살다
☐ milk	우유
☐ nice	멋진, 좋은
☐ raise	키우다, 기르다

· Unit 12 ·
Five Senses

☐ bake	(음식을) 굽다
☐ beard	턱수염
☐ cake	케이크
☐ ear	귀
☐ everything	모든 것
☐ finger	손가락
☐ grandma	할머니
☐ hear	듣다
☐ laugh	웃다; 웃음
☐ sense	감각; 감지하다
☐ smell	냄새 맡다; 냄새
☐ smile	미소 짓다; 미소
☐ sweet	달콤한
☐ taste	맛보다; 맛
☐ tongue	혀
☐ touch	만지다

1.3

미국교과서 리딩
READING

Workbook & Answer Key

길벗스쿨

미국교과서 리딩 READING

LEVEL 1 ③

Workbook

길벗스쿨

Tree House

Word Review

Ⓐ Match and trace.

1.

2.

3.

4.

many

house

hole

big

Ⓑ Look and circle.

1.  big
 squirrel

2.  animals
house

Sentence Review

A **Choose and write.**

Bees	make	house

1. We made a house in a tree.

2. Birds _____ nests in a tree.

3. _____ make hives in a tree.

B **Unscramble and write.**

1. [is] [house.] [a big] [A tree]

→ A tree is a big house.

2. [make] [in a tree.] [Spiders] [webs]

→

3. [in a tree.] [Squirrels] [holes] [make]

→

Cleaning Day

Word Review

A Match and trace.

1.

mirror

2.

bedroom

3.

clean

4.

kitchen

B Look and circle.

1.

bathroom

bedroom

2.

kitchen

living room

Sentence Review

A **Choose and write.**

clean	mirror	living room

1. I _____ the kitchen.

2. Jack cleans the _____.

3. He wipes the _____.

B **Unscramble and write.**

1. | the bedroom. | | cleans | | Mom |

   → _____

2. | mops | | He | | the floor. |

   → _____

3. | our house | | Now, | | clean! | | is |

   → _____

Safe Riding

Word Review

A Match and trace.

1.

safety

2.

helmet

3.

bike

4.

lights

B Look and circle.

1.  helmet ride

2.  knee pads lights

Sentence Review

A Choose and write.

helmet	ride	Follow

1. _____ the traffic lights.

2. Let's _____ our bikes today.

3. Put on your _____ .

B Unscramble and write.

1. | forget | | Don't | | the safety rules. |

→ _____

2. | at | | Cross | | a green light. |

→ _____

3. | your knees. | | protect | | They |

→ _____

Is a Spider an Insect?

Word Review

A Match and trace.

1.

    • three

2.

    • feeler

3.

    • wing

4.

    • think

B Look and circle.

1.

    three

    part

2.

    insects

    think

Sentence Review

A **Choose and write.**

insect	feelers	parts

1. A spider has two body _____ .

2. An _____ has wings.

3. An insect has _____ .

B **Unscramble and write.**

1. | no wings. | has | A spider |

→ _____

2. | six | has | legs. | An insect |

→ _____

3. | a spider | is | Do | think | you | an insect? |

→ _____

Different Hobbies

Word Review

Ⓐ Match and trace.

1.

2.

3.

4.

cook

story

collect

picture

Ⓑ Look and circle.

1.

story

hobby

2.

key

cook

Sentence Review

A Choose and write.

write	collecting	cook

1. He likes to _____ eggs.

2. She likes to _____ stories.

3. I enjoy _____ .

B Unscramble and write.

1. | different | have | hobbies. | We |

→ _____

2. | draw | He | pictures. | likes to |

→ _____

3. | collect | I | key rings. | like to |

→ _____

Word Review

Ⓐ Match and trace.

1.  • • listen

2.  • • sled

3.  • • scary

4.  • • give

Ⓑ Look and circle.

1.  snowman / scary

2.  long / sled

Sentence Review

A Choose and write.

giving	snowman	Winter

1. _____ is for riding.

2. Winter is for _____ .

3. We build a _____ .

B Unscramble and write.

1. | listening. | for | Winter | is |

→ _____

2. | lots of | have | snow. | We |

→ _____

3. | to friends. | give | gifts | We |

→ _____

Vegetable Face

Word Review

Ⓐ Match and trace.

1.  •

• mouth

2. 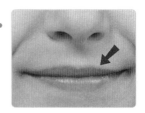 •

• hair

3.  •

• carrot

4.  •

• broccoli

Ⓑ Look and circle.

1.    broccoli

vegetables

2.    health

hair

Sentence Review

A Choose and write.

broccoli	mouth	nose

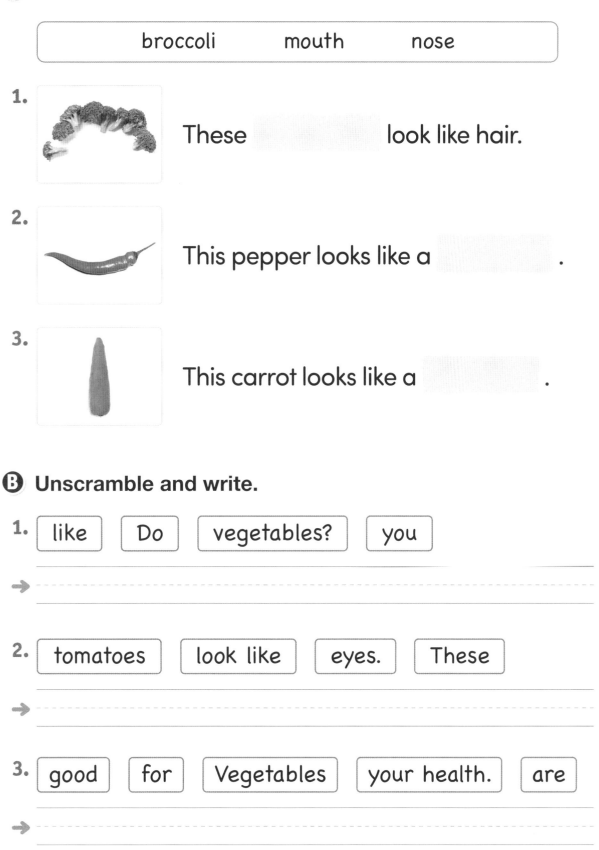

1. These _____ look like hair.

2. This pepper looks like a _____.

3. This carrot looks like a _____.

B Unscramble and write.

1. | like | Do | vegetables? | you |

→ _____

2. | tomatoes | look like | eyes. | These |

→ _____

3. | good | for | Vegetables | your health. | are |

→ _____

Word Review

Ⓐ Match and trace.

1.  •

• crab

2.  •

• fish

3.  •

• turtle

4.  •

• sea

Ⓑ Look and circle.

1.  sand

fish

2.  crab

crawl

Sentence Review

A Choose and write.

crawling	crabs	see

1. I _____ birds flying.

2. I see turtles _____ .

3. I see _____ walking sideways.

B Unscramble and write.

1. | swim | | I | | too. | | in the water, |

→ _____

2. | swimming. | | see | | fish | | I |

→ _____

3. | many | | I | | things | | do | | at the sea. |

→ _____

In My Town

Word Review

Ⓐ Match and trace.

1.

    park

2.

    town

3.

    pool

4.

    watch

Ⓑ Look and circle.

1.

    pool

    library

2.

    theater

    town

Sentence Review

A Choose and write.

park	read	theater

1. There is a _____ in my town.

2. I _____ books in the library.

3. I ride my bike in the _____ .

B Unscramble and write.

1. | a swimming pool | is | There | in | my town. |

→ _____

2. | I | the theater. | watch | in | movies |

→ _____

3. | What places | in | there | are | your town? |

→ _____

My School Tools

Word Review

Ⓐ Match and trace.

1.

   fork

2.

   cup

3.

   ruler

4.

   knife

Ⓑ Look and circle.

1.    crayons   rulers

2.    tools   cups

Sentence Review

A Choose and write.

use	art	ruler

1. In math class, I use a ____ to measure.

2. In ____ class, I use crayons to color.

3. In cooking class, I ____ a knife to cut.

B Unscramble and write.

1. | to eat. | use | a fork | I |

→ _____

2. | a pencil | to write. | use | I |

→ _____

3. | tools | at school | I | every day. | use |

→ _____

On the Farm

Word Review

Ⓐ Match and trace.

1.    •   •   duck

2.    •   •   cheese

3.    •   •   wool

4.    •   •   raise

Ⓑ Look and circle.

1.    duck   sheep

2.    feather   wool

Sentence Review

A **Choose and write.**

They	eggs	give

1. They give us fresh _____ .

2. _____ give us nice feathers.

3. They _____ us cozy wool.

B **Unscramble and write.**

1. | sheep. | My aunt | raises |

→

2. | milk | give | They | us | cheese. | and |

→

3. | We | on the farm. | raise | many animals |

→

Five Senses

Word Review

Ⓐ Match and trace.

1.

finger

2.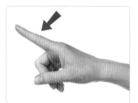

ear

3.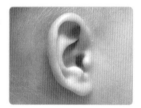

smell

4.

sweet

Ⓑ Look and circle.

1.

hear

sweet

2.

finger

taste

Sentence Review

A Choose and write.

| ears | touch | smell |

1. I hear everything with my _____ .

2. I _____ everything with my nose.

3. I _____ my dad's beard.

B Unscramble and write.

1. | I | with | my eyes. | see | everything |

→ _____

2. | my brother | hear | I | laughing. |

→ _____

3. | I | my mom's | taste | cake. | sweet |

→ _____

Workbook | 워크북 정답

Unit 1. Tree House

■ Words Review

A **1.** big   **2.** house

    3. many   **4.** hole

B **1.** squirrel   **2.** animals

■ Sentences Review

A **1.** house   **2.** make

    3. Bees

B **1.** A tree is a big house.

    2. Spiders make webs in a tree.

    3. Squirrels make holes in a tree.

Unit 2. Cleaning Day

■ Words Review

A **1.** mirror   **2.** clean

    3. kitchen   **4.** bedroom

B **1.** bathroom   **2.** living room

■ Sentences Review

A **1.** clean   **2.** living room

    3. mirror

B **1.** Mom cleans the bedroom.

    2. He mops the floor.

    3. Now, our house is clean!

Unit 3. Safe Riding

■ Words Review

A **1.** bike   **2.** helmet

    3. lights   **4.** safety

B **1.** ride   **2.** knee pads

■ Sentences Review

A **1.** Follow   **2.** ride

    3. helmet

B **1.** Don't forget the safety rules.

    2. Cross at a green light.

    3. They protect your knees.

Unit 4. Is a Spider an Insect?

■ Words Review

A **1.** three   **2.** wing

    3. feeler   **4.** think

B **1.** part   **2.** insects

■ Sentences Review

A **1.** parts   **2.** insect

    3. feelers

B **1.** A spider has no wings.

    2. An insect has six legs.

    3. Do you think a spider is an insect?

Unit 5. Different Hobbies

■ **Words Review**

A **1.** picture   **2.** cook

    3. story   **4.** collect

B **1.** hobby   **2.** key

■ **Sentences Review**

A **1.** cook   **2.** write

    3. collecting

B **1.** We have different hobbies.

    2. He likes to draw pictures.

    3. I like to collect key rings.

Unit 6. Winter Fun

■ **Words Review**

A **1.** sled   **2.** scary

    3. listen   **4.** give

B **1.** snowman   **2.** long

■ **Sentences Review**

A **1.** Winter   **2.** giving

    3. snowman

B **1.** Winter is for listening.

    2. We have lots of snow.

    3. We give gifts to friends.

Unit 7. Vegetable Face

■ **Words Review**

A **1.** broccoli   **2.** mouth

    3. hair   **4.** carrot

B **1.** vegetables   **2.** health

■ **Sentences Review**

A **1.** broccoli   **2.** mouth

    3. nose

B **1.** Do you like vegetables?

    2. These tomatoes look like eyes.

    3. Vegetables are good for your health.

Unit 8. At the Sea

■ **Words Review**

A **1.** fish   **2.** turtle

    3. crab   **4.** sea

B **1.** sand   **2.** crawl

■ **Sentences Review**

A **1.** see   **2.** crawling

    3. crabs

B **1.** I swim in the water, too.

    2. I see fish swimming.

    3. I do many things at the sea.

Unit 9. In My Town

■ **Words Review**

Ⓐ 1. watch   **2.** park

    3. pool   **4.** town

Ⓑ 1. library   **2.** theater

■ **Sentences Review**

Ⓐ 1. theater   **2.** read

    3. park

Ⓑ 1. There is a swimming pool in my town.

    2. I watch movies in the theater.

    3. What places are there in your town?

Unit 10. My School Tools

■ **Words Review**

Ⓐ 1. fork   **2.** ruler

    3. cup   **4.** knife

Ⓑ 1. crayons   **2.** tools

■ **Sentences Review**

Ⓐ 1. ruler   **2.** art

    3. use

Ⓑ 1. I use a fork to eat.

    2. I use a pencil to write.

    3. I use tools at school every day.

Unit 11. On the Farm

■ **Words Review**

Ⓐ 1. duck   **2.** cheese

    3. raise   **4.** wool

Ⓑ 1. sheep   **2.** feather

■ **Sentences Review**

Ⓐ 1. eggs   **2.** They

    3. give

Ⓑ 1. My aunt raises sheep.

    2. They give us milk and cheese.

    3. We raise many animals on the farm.

Unit 12. Five Senses

■ **Words Review**

Ⓐ 1. sweet   **2.** finger

    3. ear   **4.** smell

Ⓑ 1. hear   **2.** taste

■ **Sentences Review**

Ⓐ 1. ears   **2.** smell

    3. touch

Ⓑ 1. I see everything with my eyes.

    2. I hear my brother laughing.

    3. I taste my mom's sweet cake.

R 미국교과서 리딩
READING

LEVEL 1 ③

Answer Key

길벗스쿨

Unit 1 Tree House 나무 집

Get Ready p.10

■ **Key Words** 단어를 듣고, 알맞은 사진을 가리키세요.

big 큰   house 집   many 많은

animals 동물   squirrel 다람쥐   hole 구멍

■ **Quick Check** 알맞은 단어를 쓰세요.

animals   squirrel   hole   house

■ **Key Sentence**

Many animals make their homes in a tree.
(많은 동물들이 나무에 그들의 집을 지어요.)

듣고 따라 말한 후 알맞게 연결하세요.

Bees make hives in a tree. (벌은 나무에 벌집을 지어요.) **d**

Birds make nests in a tree. (새는 나무에 둥지를 지어요.) **c**

Squirrels make holes in a tree.
(다람쥐는 나무에 구멍을 만들어요.) **b**

Spiders make webs in a tree.
(거미는 나무에 거미줄을 쳐요.) **a**

■ **Quick Check** 알맞은 단어에 동그라미 하고 쓰세요.

Spiders make <u>webs</u> in a tree.
(거미는 나무에 거미줄을 쳐요.)

Now You Read p.12

나무 집

나무는 큰 집이에요.
많은 동물이 나무에 그들의 집을 지어요.

벌은 나무에 벌집을 지어요.
새는 나무에 둥지를 지어요.

다람쥐는 나무에 구멍을 만들어요.
거미는 나무에 거미줄을 쳐요.

보세요, 우리도 나무에 집을 지었어요.
나무는 아주 큰 집이에요.

■ **Pop Quiz**

어떤 동물이 보이나요?
새, 다람쥐, 벌, 거미(birds, squirrels, bees, and spiders)

Check Up p.14

■ **Comprehension** 다음을 읽고 알맞은 것에 체크하세요.

1. 이것은 _____에 대한 이야기예요.
   ☑ 나무 집   ☐ 거미

2. 많은 동물이 _____에 그들의 집을 지어요.
   ☐ 벌집   ☑ 나무

3. 새는 나무에 거미줄을 쳐요.   False

4. 나무는 아주 큰 집이에요.   True

■ **Sentence** 그림을 보고 문장에 알맞은 단어에 동그라미 하세요.

1. Bees make <u>hives</u> in a tree. (벌은 나무에 벌집을 지어요.)

2. Squirrels make <u>holes</u> in a tree.
   (다람쥐는 나무에 구멍을 만들어요.)

3. A tree is a very <u>big</u> house. (나무는 아주 큰 집이에요.)

■ **Word** 퍼즐을 완성하세요.

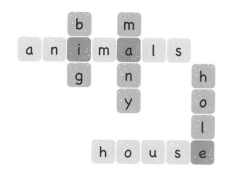

■ **Wrap-up** 그림을 보고 알맞은 단어를 쓰세요.

1. Birds make <u>nests</u> in a tree. (새는 나무에 둥지를 지어요.)

2. Spiders make <u>webs</u> in a tree.
   (거미는 나무에 거미줄을 쳐요.)

3. Bees make <u>hives</u> in a tree. (벌은 나무에 벌집을 지어요.)

4. Squirrels make <u>holes</u> in a tree.
   (다람쥐는 나무에 구멍을 만들어요.)

Unit 2 Cleaning Day 청소하는 날

p.16~21

Get Ready
p.16

- **Key Words** 단어를 듣고, 알맞은 사진을 가리키세요.

    clean 청소하다; 깨끗한   bedroom 침실   bathroom 욕실
    mirror 거울   kitchen 부엌   living room 거실

- **Quick Check** 알맞은 단어를 쓰세요.

    bathroom   clean   mirror   kitchen

- **Key Sentence**

    Mom cleans the bedroom. (엄마는 침실을 청소해요.)

듣고 따라 말한 후 알맞게 연결하세요.
Dad cleans the bathroom. (아빠는 욕실을 청소해요.) **ⓒ**
He cleans the floor. (그는 바닥을 청소해요.) **ⓓ**
She cleans the living room. (그녀는 거실을 청소해요.) **ⓑ**
I clean the kitchen. (나는 부엌을 청소해요.) **ⓐ**

- **Quick Check** 알맞은 단어에 동그라미 하고 쓰세요.

    Dad cleans the bathroom. (아빠는 욕실을 청소해요.)

Now You Read
p.18

청소하는 날

일요일 아침이에요.
우리는 오늘 바빠요.

엄마는 침실을 청소해요.
그녀는 침대를 정리해요.

아빠는 욕실을 청소해요.
그는 거울을 닦아요.

우리는 엄마와 아빠를 도와요.
나는 부엌을 청소해요.
나는 설거지를 해요.

잭은 거실을 청소해요.
그는 대걸레로 바닥을 닦아요.

이제 우리 집이 깨끗해요!

- **Pop Quiz**

    이 집에는 어떤 동물이 살고 있나요?   개(a dog)

Check Up
p.20

- **Comprehension** 다음을 읽고 알맞은 것에 체크하세요.

1. 이것은 _____에 대한 이야기예요.
    ☑ 청소   □ 이사

2. 우리는 오늘 _____.
    □ 행복해요   ☑ 바빠요

3. 아빠는 욕실을 청소해요.   True

4. 엄마는 설거지를 해요.   False

- **Sentence** 그림을 보고 문장에 알맞은 단어에 동그라미 하세요.

1. I clean the **kitchen**. (나는 부엌을 청소해요.)
2. Jack cleans the **living room**. (잭은 거실을 청소해요.)
3. Now, our house is **clean**! (이제, 우리 집이 깨끗해요!)

- **Wod** 단어를 찾아 동그라미 하세요.

b	a	t	h	r	o	o	m
c	d	e	m	n	b	o	i
v	c	l	e	a	n	s	r
b	g	d	r	o	a	m	r
p	t	o	u	y	i	m	o
k	i	t	c	h	e	n	r

- **Wrap-up** 알맞은 단어를 쓰고 관계 있는 것끼리 연결하세요.

1. Dad cleans the **bathroom**. (아빠는 욕실을 청소해요.)
    - **ⓑ** He wipes the mirror. (그는 거울을 닦아요.)
2. Mom cleans the **bedroom**. (엄마는 침실을 청소해요.)
    - **ⓐ** She makes the bed. (그녀는 침대를 정리해요.)
3. I clean the **kitchen**. (나는 부엌을 청소해요.)
    - **ⓓ** I do the dishes. (나는 설거지를 해요.)
4. Jack cleans the **living room**. (잭은 거실을 청소해요.)
    - **ⓒ** He mops the floor. (그는 대걸레로 바닥을 닦아요.)

Get Ready p.22

- **Key Words** 단어를 듣고, 알맞은 사진을 가리키세요.

  ride 타다   bike 자전거   safety 안전

  helmet 헬멧   knee pads 무릎 보호대   lights 신호등, 불빛들

- **Quick Check** 알맞은 단어를 쓰세요.

  ride   helmet   bike   lights

- **Key Sentence**

  Put on your helmet. (헬멧을 써.)

듣고 따라 말한 후 알맞게 연결하세요.

Put on your knee pads. (무릎 보호대를 착용해.) **c**

Stop at a red light. (빨간불에 멈춰.) **a**

Cross at a green light. (초록불에 건너.) **b**

Follow the traffic lights. (신호등을 지켜.) **d**

- **Quick Check** 알맞은 단어에 동그라미 하고 쓰세요.

  Put on your <u>helmet</u>. (헬멧을 써.)

Now You Read p.24

안전하게 타기

오늘은 우리 자전거를 타자.
안전 규칙을 잊지 말거라.

헬멧을 써.
그것은 너의 머리를 보호해 준단다.
무릎 보호대를 착용해.
그것들은 너의 무릎을 보호해 준단다.

신호등을 지켜.
그것들은 너를 안전하게 지켜 준다.
빨간불에 멈춰.
초록불에 건너.

오, 아빠!
조심하세요!

- **Pop Quiz**

  도로 위에 자동차가 몇 대 있나요?   세 대(three cars)

Check Up p.26

- **Comprehension** 다음을 읽고 알맞은 것에 체크하세요.

1. 이것은 _____에 대한 이야기예요.

   ☑ 안전하게 타기   ☐ 안전하게 수영하기

2. 안전 _____를(을) 잊지 말거라.

   ☐ 둥지   ☑ 규칙

3. 헬멧은 너의 머리를 보호해 준단다.   True

4. 무릎 보호대는 너의 손을 보호해 준단다.   False

- **Sentence** 그림을 보고 문장에 알맞은 단어에 동그라미 하세요.

1. Let's ride our <u>bikes</u> today. (오늘은 우리 자전거를 타자.)
2. Put on your <u>knee pads</u>. (무릎 보호대를 착용해.)
3. Stop at a <u>red</u> light. (빨간불에 멈춰.)

- **Word** 퍼즐을 완성하세요.

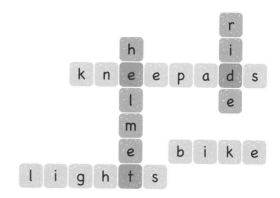

- **Wrap-up** 관계 있는 것끼리 연결하고 알맞은 단어를 쓰세요.

1. They keep you safe. (그것들은 너를 안전하게 지켜 준단다.)
   - **c** traffic <u>lights</u> (신호등)
2. It protects your head. (그것은 너의 머리를 보호해 준단다.)
   - **b** <u>helmet</u> (헬멧)
3. They protect your knees. (그것들은 너의 무릎을 보호해 준단다.)
   - **a** <u>knee pads</u> (무릎 보호대)

Get Ready
p.28

- **Key Words** 단어를 듣고, 알맞은 사진을 가리키세요.

  insects 곤충들   three 3, 셋   part 부분

  wing 날개   feeler 더듬이   think 생각하다

- **Quick Check** 알맞은 단어를 쓰세요.

  insects   wing   feeler   think

- **Key Sentence**

  A spider has two body parts.
  (거미는 몸이 두 부분으로 되어 있어요.)

듣고 따라 말한 후 알맞게 연결하세요.

An insect has six legs. (곤충은 여섯 개의 다리가 있어요.) **d**

An insect has wings. (곤충은 날개가 있어요.) **c**

An insect has three body parts.
(곤충은 몸이 세 부분으로 되어 있어요.) **b**

A spider has eight legs. (거미는 여덟 개의 다리가 있어요.) **a**

- **Quick Check** 알맞은 단어에 동그라미 하고 쓰세요.

  An insect has <u>wings</u>. (곤충은 날개가 있어요.)

Now You Read
p.30

거미는 곤충일까요?

곤충은 몸이 세 부분으로 되어 있어요.
거미는 몸이 두 부분으로 되어 있어요.

곤충은 날개가 있어요.
거미는 날개가 없어요.

곤충은 여섯 개의 다리가 있어요.
거미는 여덟 개의 다리가 있어요.

곤충은 더듬이가 있어요.
거미는 더듬이가 없어요.

당신은 거미가 곤충이라고 생각하나요?

- **Pop Quiz**

  거미줄 위에는 무엇이 있나요?   거미(a spider)

Check Up
p.32

- **Comprehension** 다음을 읽고 알맞은 것에 체크하세요.

1. 이것은 _____에 대한 이야기예요.
   ☑ 거미   ☐ 나비

2. 거미는 몸이 _____ 부분으로 되어 있어요.
   ☑ 두   ☐ 세

3. 곤충은 몸이 세 부분으로 되어 있어요.   True

4. 거미는 곤충이에요.   False

- **Sentence** 그림을 보고 문장에 알맞은 단어에 동그라미 하세요.

1. An insect has <u>wings</u>. (곤충은 날개가 있어요.)
2. A spider has eight <u>legs</u>. (거미는 여덟 개의 다리가 있어요.)
3. Do you <u>think</u> a spider is an insect?
   (당신은 거미가 곤충이라고 생각하나요?)

- **Word** 단어를 찾아 동그라미 하세요.

t	a	m	f	f	e	b	c
h	j	p	e	e	x	z	w
i	n	s	e	c	t	s	a
n	t	q	l	l	x	d	b
k	g	q	e	e	e	g	c
o	p	a	r	t	c	i	m

- **Wrap-up** 그림을 보고 관련 있는 것에 연결하세요.

1. A spider has _____. (거미는 ~을 가지고 있어요.)
   two body parts (두 부분으로 된 몸), **eight legs** (다리 8개)
2. An insect has _____. (곤충은 ~을 가지고 있어요.)
   three body parts (세 부분으로 된 몸), **six legs** (다리 6개),
   wings (날개), **feelers** (더듬이)

Get Ready p.34

■ **Key Words** 단어를 듣고, 알맞은 사진을 가리키세요.

hobby 취미   cook 요리하다   story 이야기

picture 그림   collect 모으다   key 열쇠

■ **Quick Check** 알맞은 단어를 쓰세요.

cook   story   key   picture

■ **Key Sentence**

He likes to cook eggs. (그는 달걀 요리하는 것을 좋아해요.)

듣고 따라 말한 후 알맞게 연결하세요.

She likes to write stories. (그녀는 이야기 쓰는 것을 좋아해요.) **d**

He likes to draw pictures. (그는 그림 그리는 것을 좋아해요.) **b**

He likes to read books. (그는 책 읽는 것을 좋아해요.) **a**

I like to collect key rings.

(나는 열쇠고리 모으는 것을 좋아해요.) **c**

■ **Quick Check** 알맞은 단어에 동그라미 하고 쓰세요.

She likes to write stories. (그녀는 이야기 쓰는 것을 좋아해요.)

Now You Read p.36

여러 가지 취미

모든 사람은 취미가 있어요.
취미는 우리에게 기쁨을 가져다줘요.

지미는 요리를 즐겨요.
그는 달걀 요리하는 것을 좋아해요.

애나는 글쓰기를 즐겨요.
그녀는 이야기 쓰는 것을 좋아해요.

데이빗은 그리기를 즐겨요.
그는 그림 그리는 것을 좋아해요.

나는 모으기를 즐겨요.
나는 열쇠고리 모으는 것을 좋아해요.

우리는 다른 취미를 가지고 있어요.
당신의 취미는 무엇인가요?

■ **Pop Quiz**

남자아이는 무엇을 그리고 있나요?   성(a castle)

Check Up p.38

■ **Comprehension** 다음을 읽고 알맞은 것에 체크하세요.

1. 이것은 _____에 대한 이야기예요.
   ☑ 취미들   □ 그림들

2. 취미는 우리에게 _____을 가져다줘요.
   □ 안전   ☑ 기쁨

3. 지미는 글쓰기를 즐겨요.   False

4. 우리는 다른 취미를 가지고 있어요.   True

■ **Sentence** 그림을 보고 문장에 알맞은 단어에 동그라미 하세요.

1. Anna likes to write stories. (애나는 이야기 쓰는 것을 좋아해요.)
2. David enjoys drawing. (데이빗은 그리기를 즐겨요.)
3. I like to collect key rings.
   (나는 열쇠고리 모으는 것을 좋아해요.)

■ **Word** 퍼즐을 완성하세요.

■ **Wrap-up** 그림을 보고 알맞은 단어를 쓰세요.

1. Jimmy likes to cook eggs. (지미는 달걀 요리하는 것을 좋아해요.)
2. David likes to draw pictures.
   (데이빗은 그림 그리는 것을 좋아해요.)
3. I like to collect key rings.
   (나는 열쇠고리 모으는 것을 좋아해요.)
4. Anna likes to write stories. (애나는 이야기 쓰는 것을 좋아해요.)

Unit 6 Winter Fun 겨울의 재미

Get Ready
p.40

- **Key Words** 단어를 듣고, 알맞은 사진을 가리키세요.

  sled 썰매; 썰매를 타다　snowman 눈사람　listen 듣다

  long 긴　　　　　　scary 무서운　　give 주다

- **Quick Check** 알맞은 단어를 쓰세요.

  listen　　sled　　long　　snowman

- **Key Sentence**

  Winter is for riding. (겨울은 타기 위한 계절이에요.)

듣고 따라 말한 후 알맞게 연결하세요.

Winter is for building. (겨울은 만들기 위한 계절이에요.) **c**

Winter is for listening. (겨울은 듣기 위한 계절이에요.) **b**

Winter is for giving. (겨울은 주기 위한 계절이에요.) **d**

Winter is for skating. (겨울은 스케이트를 타기 위한 계절이에요.) **a**

- **Quick Check** 알맞은 단어에 동그라미 하고 쓰세요.

  Winter is for building. (겨울은 만들기 위한 계절이에요.)

Now You Read
p.42

겨울의 재미

겨울은 타기 위한 계절이에요.
우리는 언덕 아래로 썰매를 타요.
우리는 하루 종일 썰매를 타요.

겨울은 만들기 위한 계절이에요.
우리는 많은 눈을 가져요.
우리는 눈사람을 만들어요.

겨울은 듣기 위한 계절이에요.
밤이 길어요.
우리는 무서운 이야기를 들어요.

겨울은 주기 위한 계절이에요.
크리스마스가 겨울에 있어요.
우리는 친구들에게 선물을 줘요.

겨울은 아주 재미있어요!

- **Pop Quiz**

  눈사람은 무엇을 입고 있나요?
  모자와 목도리(a hat and a muffler)

Check Up
p.44

- **Comprehension** 다음을 읽고 알맞은 것에 체크하세요.

1. 이것은 _____에 대한 이야기예요.
   □ 눈　　　　　　　✔ 겨울

2. 우리는 하루 종일 _____.
   ✔ 썰매를 타요　　　□ 잠을 자요

3. 겨울은 만들기 위한 계절이에요.　　　　True

4. 겨울에는 밤이 짧아요.　　　　　　　　False

- **Sentence** 그림을 보고 문장에 알맞은 단어에 동그라미 하세요.

1. Winter is for listening. (겨울은 듣기 위한 계절이에요.)

2. We build a snowman. (우리는 눈사람을 만들어요.)

3. Winter is for riding. (겨울은 타기 위한 계절이에요.)

- **Word** 단어를 찾아 동그라미 하세요.

s	b	a	d	a	m	l	e
c	o	e	e	w	f	e	v
a	r	t	s	c	a	t	s
r	g	i	v	e	p	a	f
y	o	r	w	s	l	e	d
s	n	o	w	m	a	n	s

- **Wrap-up** 그림을 보고 알맞은 단어를 쓰세요.

1. We build a snowman. (우리는 눈사람을 만들어요.)

2. We listen to scary stories. (우리는 무서운 이야기를 들어요.)

3. We sled all day long. (우리는 하루 종일 썰매를 타요.)

4. We give gifts to friends. (우리는 친구들에게 선물을 줘요.)

Unit 7 Vegetable Face 채소 얼굴

p.46~51

Get Ready
p.46

■ **Key Words** 단어를 듣고, 알맞은 사진을 가리키세요.

vegetables 채소	broccoli 브로콜리	hair 머리카락
carrot 당근	mouth 입	health 건강

■ **Quick Check** 알맞은 단어를 쓰세요.

hair   carrot   mouth   health

■ **Key Sentence**

These tomatoes look like eyes.
(이 토마토는 눈처럼 생겼어요.)

듣고 따라 말한 후 알맞게 연결하세요.

These broccoli look like hair.
(이 브로콜리는 머리카락처럼 생겼어요.) **d**
This corn looks like teeth. (이 옥수수는 이처럼 생겼어요.) **b**
This pepper looks like a mouth.
(이 고추는 입처럼 생겼어요.) **a**
This carrot looks like a nose. (이 당근은 코처럼 생겼어요.) **c**

■ **Quick Check** 알맞은 단어에 동그라미 하고 쓰세요.

This carrot looks like a nose. (이 당근은 코처럼 생겼어요.)

Now You Read
p.48

채소 얼굴

채소를 좋아하나요?
"아니요."
채소를 안 좋아한다고요?

채소는 건강에 좋아요.
그리고 재미있게 생겼지요!

봐요! 여기 내 작품이 있어요!
이 토마토는 눈처럼 생겼어요.
이 브로콜리는 머리카락처럼 생겼어요.
이 당근은 코처럼 생겼어요.
이 고추는 입처럼 생겼어요.

나는 채소를 아주 많이 좋아해요!

■ **Pop Quiz**

채소 얼굴에서 코는 무엇으로 만들었나요?   당근(a carrot)

Check Up
p.50

■ **Comprehension** 다음을 읽고 알맞은 것에 체크하세요.

1. 이것은 _____에 대한 이야기예요.
   ☑ 채소   ☐ 얼굴

2. 채소는 당신의 _____에 좋아요.
   ☐ 집   ☑ 건강

3. 이 토마토는 코처럼 생겼어요.   False

4. 이 고추는 입처럼 생겼어요.   True

■ **Sentence** 그림을 보고 문장에 알맞은 단어에 동그라미 하세요.

1. This carrot looks like a <u>nose</u>. (이 당근은 코처럼 생겼어요.)
2. These broccoli look like <u>hair</u>.
   (이 브로콜리는 머리카락처럼 생겼어요.)
3. Vegetables look <u>funny</u>! (채소는 재미있게 생겼어요!)

■ **Word** 퍼즐을 완성하세요.

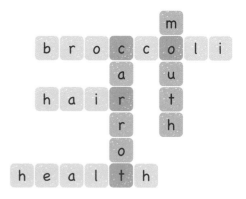

■ **Wrap-up** 그림을 보고 알맞은 단어를 쓰세요.

1. These <u>broccoli</u> look like hair.
   (이 브로콜리는 머리카락처럼 생겼어요.)
2. These <u>tomatoes</u> look like eyes. (이 토마토는 눈처럼 생겼어요.)
3. This <u>carrot</u> looks like a nose. (이 당근은 코처럼 생겼어요.)
4. This <u>pepper</u> looks like a mouth. (이 고추는 입처럼 생겼어요.)

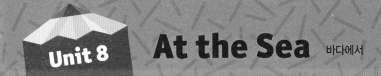
Get Ready
p.52

■ **Key Words** 단어를 듣고, 알맞은 사진을 가리키세요.

sea 바다	turtle 거북이	crawl 기어가다
sand 모래	fish 물고기	crab 게

■ **Quick Check** 알맞은 단어를 쓰세요.

sand　　　fish　　　turtle　　　crab

■ **Key Sentence**

I see birds flying. (나는 새가 날아가고 있는 것을 봐요.)

듣고 따라 말한 후 알맞게 연결하세요.

I see turtles crawling. (나는 거북이가 기어가고 있는 것을 봐요.) **ⓑ**
I see fish swimming. (나는 물고기가 수영하고 있는 것을 봐요.) **ⓐ**
I see crabs walking sideways.
(나는 게가 옆으로 걷고 있는 것을 봐요.) **ⓓ**
I see clouds moving. (나는 구름이 움직이고 있는 것을 봐요.) **ⓒ**

■ **Quick Check** 알맞은 단어에 동그라미 하고 쓰세요.

I see turtles crawling.

(나는 거북이가 기어가고 있는 것을 봐요.)

Now You Read
p.54

바다에서

나는 바다에서 많은 것을 봐요.
나는 바다에서 많은 일을 해요.

나는 새가 날아가고 있는 것을 봐요.
나도 하늘을 날아요.

나는 거북이가 기어가고 있는 것을 봐요.
나도 모래에서 기어요.

나는 물고기가 수영하고 있는 것을 봐요.
나도 물속에서 수영해요.

나는 게가 옆으로 걷고 있는 것을 봐요.
나도 옆으로 걸어요.
아야!

■ **Pop Quiz**

조개껍데기가 몇 개 보이나요?　　네 개(four seashells)

Check Up
p.56

■ **Comprehension** 다음을 읽고 알맞은 것에 체크하세요.

1. 이것은 _____에 있는 많은 것들에 대한 이야기예요.
   □ 언덕　　　　　　　✓ 바다

2. 나는 새가 _____을 봐요.
   ✓ 날아가고 있는 것　　　□ 달리고 있는 것

3. 나는 바다에서 많은 일들을 해요.　　　　　　True

4. 나도 물속에서 날아요.　　　　　　　　　　False

■ **Sentence** 그림을 보고 문장에 알맞은 단어에 동그라미 하세요.

1. I see fish **swimming**. (나는 물고기들이 수영하고 있는 것을 봐요.)
2. I crawl in the **sand**, too. (나도 모래에서 기어요.)
3. I see **crabs** walking sideways.
   (나는 게들이 옆으로 걷고 있는 것을 봐요.)

■ **Word** 단어를 찾아 동그라미 하세요.

g	i	w	d	c	r	a	b
t	j	s	d	r	x	c	n
h	d	c	s	a	n	d	q
s	a	n	o	w	d	p	o
e	w	f	a	l	x	v	a
a	i	o	w	s	x	c	n

■ **Wrap-up** 관계 있는 것끼리 연결하고 알맞은 단어를 쓰세요.

1. **ⓑ** I see birds **flying**. (나는 새가 날아가고 있는 것을 봐요.)
2. **ⓒ** I see turtles **crawling**.
   (나는 거북이가 기어가고 있는 것을 봐요.)
3. **ⓓ** I see fish **swimming**.
   (나는 물고기가 수영하고 있는 것을 봐요.)
4. **ⓐ** I see crabs **walking** sideways.
   (나는 게가 옆으로 걷고 있는 것을 봐요.)

Get Ready   p.58

■ **Key Words** 단어를 듣고, 알맞은 사진을 가리키세요.

library 도서관   town 동네, 마을   theater 극장

watch 보다   park 공원   pool 수영장

■ **Quick Check** 알맞은 단어를 쓰세요.

watch   park   town   pool

■ **Key Sentence**

There is a library in my town. (우리 동네에는 도서관이 있어요.)

듣고 따라 말한 후 알맞게 연결하세요.

There is a theater in my town. (우리 동네에는 극장이 있어요.) ⓓ

There is a park in my town. (우리 동네에는 공원이 있어요.) ⓐ

There is a swimming pool in my town.
(우리 동네에는 수영장이 있어요.) ⓑ

There is a museum in my town.
(우리 동네에는 박물관이 있어요.) ⓒ

■ **Quick Check** 알맞은 단어에 동그라미 하고 쓰세요.

There is a <u>theater</u> in my town. (우리 동네에는 극장이 있어요.)

Now You Read   p.60

우리 동네에는

우리 동네에는 도서관이 있어요.
나는 도서관에서 책을 읽어요.

우리 동네에는 극장이 있어요.
나는 극장에서 영화를 봐요.

우리 동네에는 공원이 있어요.
나는 공원에서 자전거를 타요.

우리 동네에는 수영장이 있어요.
나는 매일 수영장에서 수영을 해요.

당신의 동네에는 어떤 곳이 있나요?

■ **Pop Quiz**

아이들 몇 명이 수영장에서 수영하고 있나요?

네 명(four children)

Check Up   p.62

■ **Comprehension** 다음을 읽고 알맞은 것에 체크하세요.

1. 이것은 _____에 대한 이야기예요.
  □ 우리 집   ☑ 우리 동네

2. 나는 _____에서 책을 읽어요.
  ☑ 도서관   □ 수영장

3. 우리 동네에는 공원이 있어요.   True

4. 나는 극장에서 수영을 해요.   False

■ **Sentence** 그림을 보고 문장에 알맞은 단어에 동그라미 하세요.

1. There is a <u>library</u> in my town. (우리 동네에는 도서관이 있어요.)

2. There is a <u>swimming pool</u> in my town.
  (우리 동네에는 수영장이 있어요.)

3. I ride my <u>bike</u> in the park. (나는 공원에서 자전거를 타요.)

■ **Word** 퍼즐을 완성하세요.

■ **Wrap-up** 관계 있는 것끼리 연결하고 알맞은 단어를 쓰세요.

1. I watch movies in the <u>theater</u>.
  (나는 극장에서 영화를 봐요.) ⓑ

2. I swim in the <u>pool</u>. (나는 수영장에서 수영을 해요.) ⓓ

3. I read books in the <u>library</u>. (나는 도서관에서 책을 읽어요.) ⓐ

4. I ride my bike in the <u>park</u>. (나는 공원에서 자전거를 타요.) ⓒ

Get Ready

p.64

- **Key Words** 단어를 듣고, 알맞은 사진을 가리키세요.

  tools 도구   ruler 자   crayons 크레용

  knife 칼   fork 포크   cup 컵

- **Quick Check** 알맞은 단어를 쓰세요.

  tools   crayons   fork   cup

- **Key Sentence**

  I use a ruler to measure.

  (나는 길이를 재기 위해서 자를 사용해요.)

듣고 따라 말한 후 알맞게 연결하세요.

I use a pencil to write. (나는 쓰기 위해서 연필을 사용해요.) **ⓒ**

I use crayons to color.

(나는 색칠하기 위해서 크레용을 사용해요.) **ⓑ**

I use a knife to cut. (나는 자르기 위해서 칼을 사용해요.) **ⓐ**

I use a cup to drink. (나는 마시기 위해서 컵을 사용해요.) **ⓓ**

- **Quick Check** 알맞은 단어에 동그라미 하고 쓰세요.

  I use a <u>ruler</u> to measure.

  (나는 길이를 재기 위해서 자를 사용해요.)

Now You Read

p.66

나의 학교 도구

나는 매일 학교에서 도구를 사용해요.

수학 시간에 나는 길이를 재기 위해서 자를 사용해요.
작문 시간에 나는 쓰기 위해서 연필을 사용해요.

미술 시간에 나는 색칠하기 위해서 크레용을 사용해요.
요리 시간에 나는 자르기 위해서 칼을 사용해요.

점심 시간에도 나는 많은 도구를 사용해요.
나는 먹기 위해서 포크를 사용해요.
나는 마시기 위해서 컵을 사용해요.

- **Pop Quiz**

  아이는 무엇을 자르고 있나요?   당근(a carrot)

Check Up

p.68

- **Comprehension** 다음을 읽고 알맞은 것에 체크하세요.

1. 이것은 _____에 대한 이야기예요.

   ☑ 학교 도구   ☐ 수업

2. 나는 매일 _____에서 도구들을 사용해요.

   ☐ 공원   ☑ 학교

3. 나는 길이를 재기 위해서 자를 사용해요.   True

4. 나는 자르기 위해서 크레용을 사용해요.   False

- **Sentence** 그림을 보고 문장에 알맞은 단어에 동그라미 하세요.

1. I use a <u>knife</u> to cut. (나는 자르기 위해서 칼을 사용해요.)

2. I use a <u>cup</u> to drink. (나는 마시기 위해서 컵을 사용해요.)

3. At lunch time, I use many <u>tools</u>, too.

   (점심 시간에도, 나는 많은 도구를 사용해요.)

- **Word** 단어를 찾아 동그라미 하세요.

k	n	i	f	e	c	p	t
z	x	n	b	f	h	p	o
x	a	p	c	x	p	c	o
p	a	b	u	l	t	r	l
x	t	v	p	v	b	y	s
c	r	a	y	o	n	s	n

- **Wrap-up** 알맞은 단어를 쓰고 관계 있는 것끼리 연결하세요.

1. I use **crayons** to color. **ⓒ**

   (나는 색칠하기 위해서 크레용들을 사용해요.)

2. I use a <u>fork</u> to eat. **ⓐ** (나는 먹기 위해서 포크를 사용해요.)

3. I use a <u>pencil</u> to write. **ⓓ** (나는 쓰기 위해서 연필을 사용해요.)

4. I use a <u>cup</u> to drink. **ⓑ** (나는 마시기 위해서 컵을 사용해요.)

Get Ready　　　　　p.70

■ **Key Words** 단어를 듣고, 알맞은 사진을 가리키세요.

raise 키우다, 기르다　　cheese 치즈　　duck 오리

feather 깃털　　　　sheep 양　　wool 양털

■ **Quick Check** 알맞은 단어를 쓰세요.

duck　　sheep　　feather　　wool

■ **Key Sentence**

They give us milk. (그들은 우리에게 우유를 줘요.)

듣고 따라 말한 후 알맞게 연결하세요.

They give us cheese. (그들은 우리에게 치즈를 줘요.) **ⓑ**

They give us fresh eggs. (그들은 우리에게 신선한 달걀을 줘요.) **ⓐ**

They give us nice feathers. (그들은 우리에게 좋은 깃털을 줘요.) **ⓓ**

They give us cozy wool. (그들은 우리에게 포근한 양털을 줘요.) **ⓒ**

■ **Quick Check** 알맞은 단어에 동그라미 하고 쓰세요.

They give us fresh eggs. (그들은 우리에게 신선한 달걀을 줘요.)

Now You Read　　　　　p.72

농장에서

우리는 농장 가족이에요.
우리는 농장에서 많은 동물을 키워요.

우리 아빠는 젖소를 키워요.
그들은 우리에게 우유와 치즈를 줘요.

우리 엄마는 암탉을 키워요.
그들은 우리에게 신선한 달걀을 줘요.

우리 이모(고모)는 양을 키워요.
그들은 우리에게 포근한 양털을 줘요.

그리고 나는 오리를 키워요.
그들은 우리에게 좋은 깃털을 줘요.

우리는 많은 동물과 함께 농장에서 살아요.

■ **Pop Quiz**

달걀이 몇 개 보이나요?　　　　**일곱 개(seven eggs)**

Check Up　　　　　p.74

■ **Comprehension** 다음을 읽고 알맞은 것에 체크하세요.

1. 이것은 _____에 대한 이야기예요.
　　□ 음식　　　　　☑ 농장

2. 우리는 농장에서 많은 동물들을 _____.
　　☑ 키워요　　　　　□ 줘요

3. 우리 아빠는 젖소를 키워요.　　　　True

4. 우리는 도시에서 살아요.　　　　False

■ **Sentence** 그림을 보고 문장에 알맞은 단어에 동그라미 하세요.

1. Ducks give us nice <u>feathers</u>.
　　(오리는 우리에게 좋은 깃털을 줘요.)

2. My aunt raises <u>sheep</u>. (우리 이모(고모)는 양을 키워요.)

3. Cows give us <u>cheese</u>. (젖소는 우리에게 치즈를 줘요.)

■ **Word** 퍼즐을 완성하세요.

■ **Wrap-up** 관계 있는 것끼리 연결하고 알맞은 단어를 쓰세요.

1. **ⓒ** Ducks give us nice <u>feathers</u>.
　　(오리는 우리에게 좋은 깃털을 줘요.)

2. **ⓑ** Cows give us <u>milk</u> and <u>cheese</u>.
　　(젖소는 우리에게 우유와 치즈를 줘요.)

3. **ⓓ** Sheep give us cozy <u>wool</u>.
　　(양은 우리에게 포근한 양털을 줘요.)

4. **ⓐ** Hens give us fresh <u>eggs</u>.
　　(암탉은 우리에게 신선한 달걀을 줘요.)

Unit 12 Five Senses 다섯 가지 감각

Get Ready p.76

- **Key Words** 단어를 듣고, 알맞은 사진을 가리키세요.

  hear 듣다   ear 귀   smell 냄새 맡다
  finger 손가락   taste 맛보다   sweet 달콤한

- **Quick Check** 알맞은 단어를 쓰세요.

  ear   smell   taste   finger

- **Key Sentence**

  I see everything with my eyes. (나는 눈으로 모든 것을 봐요.)

듣고 따라 말한 후 알맞게 연결하세요.

I hear everything with my ears. (나는 귀로 모든 것을 들어요.) ⓐ

I smell everything with my nose.
(나는 코로 모든 것을 냄새 맡아요.) ⓒ

I touch everything with my fingers.
(나는 손가락으로 모든 것을 만져요.) ⓓ

I taste everything with my tongue.
(나는 혀로 모든 것을 맛봐요.) ⓑ

- **Quick Check** 알맞은 단어에 동그라미 하고 쓰세요.

  I <u>taste</u> everything with my tongue.
  (나는 혀로 모든 것을 맛봐요.)

Now You Read p.78

다섯 가지 감각

나는 눈으로 모든 것을 봐요.
나는 우리 할머니가 미소 짓는 것을 봐요.

나는 귀로 모든 것을 들어요.
나는 우리 남동생이 웃는 것을 들어요.

나는 코로 모든 것을 냄새 맡아요.
나는 우리 엄마가 빵을 굽는 냄새를 맡아요.

나는 손가락으로 모든 것을 만져요.
나는 우리 아빠의 수염을 만져요.

나는 혀로 모든 것을 맛봐요.
나는 우리 엄마의 달콤한 케이크를 맛봐요.

- **Pop Quiz**

  케이크 위에는 어떤 과일이 있나요?   딸기(a strawberry)

Check Up p.80

- **Comprehension** 다음을 읽고 알맞은 것에 체크하세요.

1. 이것은 다섯 가지 _____에 대한 이야기예요.
   ☑ 감각   ☐ 손가락

2. 나는 _____(으)로 모든 것을 봐요.
   ☐ 귀   ☑ 눈

3. 나는 우리 남동생이 웃는 것을 들어요.   True

4. 나는 눈으로 모든 것을 냄새 맡아요.   False

- **Sentence** 그림을 보고 문장에 알맞은 단어에 동그라미 하세요.

1. I taste everything with my <u>tongue</u>.
   (나는 혀로 모든 것을 맛봐요.)

2. I touch everything with my <u>fingers</u>.
   (나는 손가락으로 모든 것을 만져요.)

3. I <u>smell</u> my mom baking bread.
   (나는 우리 엄마가 빵을 굽는 냄새를 맡아요.)

- **Word** 단어를 찾아 동그라미 하세요.

s	w	e	e	t	s	o	x
e	b	s	d	e	m	n	g
b	f	i	n	g	e	r	c
x	e	b	c	d	l	w	e
p	d	e	d	n	l	w	a
h	a	s	t	a	w	d	r

- **Wrap-up** 그림을 보고 알맞은 단어를 쓰세요.

1. I <u>touch</u> everything with my fingers.
   (나는 손가락으로 모든 것을 만져요.)

2. I <u>see</u> everything with my eyes. (나는 눈으로 모든 것을 봐요.)

3. I <u>hear</u> everything with my ears. (나는 귀로 모든 것을 들어요.)

4. I <u>smell</u> everything with my nose.
   (나는 코로 모든 것을 냄새 맡아요.)

5. I <u>taste</u> everything with my tongue. (나는 혀로 모든 것을 맛봐요.)

미국교과서 READING Level 1 권별 리딩 주제

1권 1.1

1. Body Parts
2. My Brother
3. Family
4. My School
5. Animals
6. Seasons
7. Things in the Sky
8. Shapes
9. Clothes
10. Monsters
11. Jobs
12. Museum

2권 1.2

1. Rain
2. Spring
3. Things in Pairs
4. Animal Homes
5. Community
6 My Room
7. Bad Dream
8. Colors
9. Food
10. Transportation
11. Friends
12. Sense of Touch

3권 1.3

1. Tree
2. Housework
3. Riding a Bike
4. Spider
5. Hobbies
6. Winter
7. Vegetables
8. Sea
9. My Town
10. School Tools
11. Farm Animals
12. Five Senses

길벗스쿨 공식 카페, <기적의 공부방>에서 함께 공부해요!

기적의 학습단

홈스쿨링 응원 프로젝트! 학습단에 참여하여 공부 습관도 기르고 칭찬 선물도 받으세요!

도서 서평단

길벗스쿨의 책을 가장 먼저 체험하고, 기획에도 직접 참여해 보세요.

알찬 학습 팁

엄마표 학습 노하우를 나누며 우리 아이 맞춤 학습법을 함께 찾아요.

<기적의 공부방> https://cafe.naver.com/gilbutschool